D1064173

SandCastle™
Signs of the Seasons

SIGNS OF
Spring

Colleen Dolphin

Consulting Editor,
Diane Craig, M.A./Reading Specialist

A Division of ABDO
ABDO
Publishing Company

visit us at www.abdopublishing.com

Published by ABDO Publishing Company, a division of ABDO, P.O. Box 398166, Minneapolis, Minnesota 55439. Copyright © 2013 by Abdo Consulting Group, Inc. International copyrights reserved in all countries. No part of this book may be reproduced in any form without written permission from the publisher. SandCastle™ is a trademark and logo of ABDO Publishing Company.

Printed in the United States of America, North Mankato, Minnesota
062012
092012

 PRINTED ON RECYCLED PAPER

Editor: Liz Salzmann
Content Developer: Nancy Tuminelly
Cover and Interior Design and Production: Colleen Dolphin, Mighty Media, Inc.
Photo Credits: Holly Bergstrom, Shutterstock

Library of Congress Cataloging-in-Publication Data
Dolphin, Colleen, 1979-
 Signs of spring / Colleen Dolphin.
   p. cm. -- (Signs of the seasons)
 ISBN 978-1-61783-393-9
 1. Spring--Juvenile literature. 2. Seasons--Juvenile literature. I. Title.
 QB637.5.D65 2013
 508.2--dc23
                               2011051126

SandCastle™ Level: Beginning

SandCastle™ books are created by a team of professional educators, reading specialists, and content developers around five essential components—phonemic awareness, phonics, vocabulary, text comprehension, and fluency—to assist young readers as they develop reading skills and strategies and increase their general knowledge. All books are written, reviewed, and leveled for guided reading, early reading intervention, and Accelerated Reader® programs for use in shared, guided, and independent reading and writing activities to support a balanced approach to literacy instruction. The SandCastle™ series has four levels that correspond to early literacy development. The levels are provided to help teachers and parents select appropriate books for young readers.

Emerging Readers (no flags)   Beginning Readers (1 flag)   Transitional Readers (2 flags)   Fluent Readers (3 flags)

contents

seasons

There are four seasons during the year. They are called spring, summer, autumn, and winter. The weather, plants, animals, and daylight hours **change** during each season.

spring

summer

winter

autumn

spring

During the year, Earth travels around the sun. This brings some parts of Earth closer to the sun. Other parts of Earth get farther from the sun. Spring happens in the parts that are moving closer to the sun.

DID YOU KNOW?
In Japan it is spring in March. In Argentina it is spring in September.

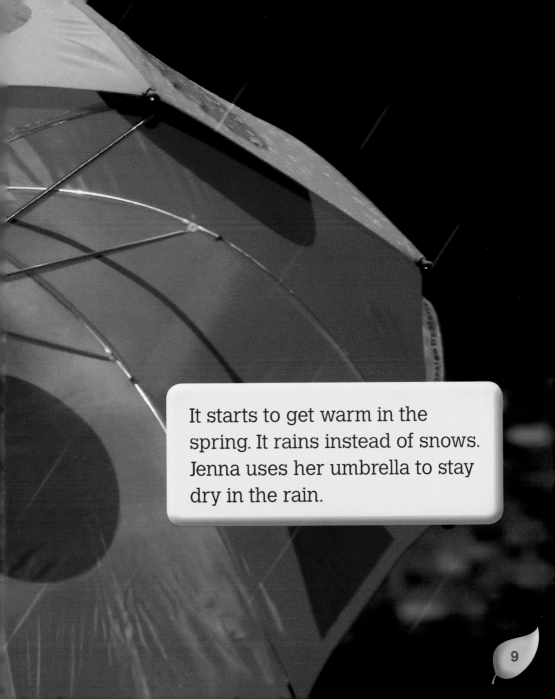

It starts to get warm in the spring. It rains instead of snows. Jenna uses her umbrella to stay dry in the rain.

After a storm there can still be
some raindrops in the sky.
The sun shines on the raindrops.
This makes a colorful **rainbow**!

The rain and warm weather help plants grow in the spring. Flowers begin to **bloom**.

DID YOU KNOW?
Tulips are spring flowers. They are one of the first flowers to bloom.

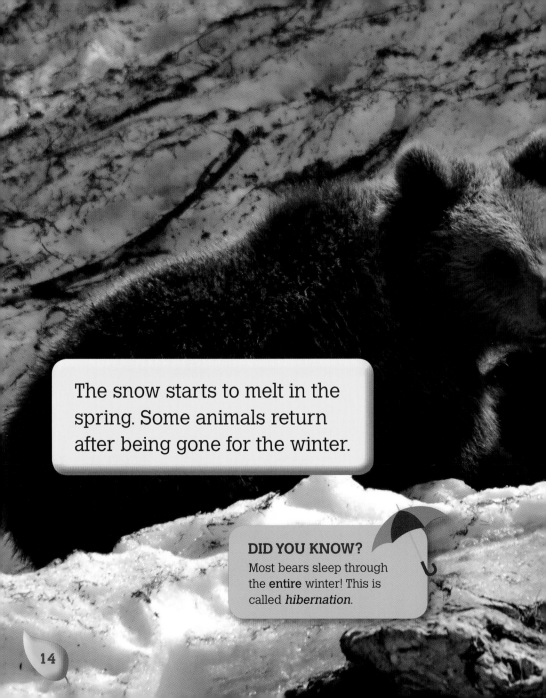

The snow starts to melt in the spring. Some animals return after being gone for the winter.

DID YOU KNOW?
Most bears sleep through the **entire** winter! This is called *hibernation*.

Many baby animals are born in the spring. They like to play in the new grass.

In the spring, there is more daylight than in the winter. Ben loves to play in the park after school.

DID YOU KNOW?
Spring comes after winter and before summer.

Henry likes to splash in **puddles** in the spring. What do you like to do? Do you play outside more when it gets warmer?

spring activities

DO SOME BIRDWATCHING!

HAVE A PICNIC!

RELAX ON A TIRE SWING!

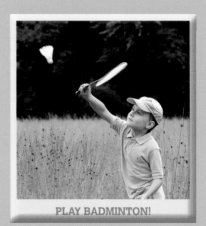

PLAY BADMINTON!

spring quiz

Read each sentence below. Then decide if it is true or false.

1. Spring is colder than winter.
   True or False?

2. Plants do not grow in the spring.
   True or False?

3. Snow starts to melt in the spring.
   True or False?

4. Many baby animals are born in the spring.
   True or False?

5. There is more daylight in the winter than in the spring. True or False?

glossary

bloom – to produce flowers.

change – to be altered or become different.

entire – whole, complete, or total.

hibernation – when an animal spends the winter in a deep sleep.

puddle – a small pool of water or other liquid.

rainbow – an arc or circle of colors caused by the sun shining through raindrops, spray, or mist.